Sounds of the Eternal:
A Celtic Psalter

Sounds of the Eternal:
A Celtic Psalter

Morning and Night Prayer

J. Philip Newell

William B. Eerdmans Publishing Company
Grand Rapids, Michigan / Cambridge, U.K.

To Jane Blaffer Owen
and her vision of a new harmony

© J. Philip Newell 2002

Illustrations from Hebrew Illuminated Manuscripts by
permission of the British Library

First published 2002 in the U.K. by
The Canterbury Press, Norwich

This edition published 2002 in the U.S.A. by
Wm. B. Eerdmans Publishing Company
255 Jefferson Ave. SE, Grand Rapids, Michigan 49503
www.eerdmans.com

Library of Congress Cataloging-in-Publication Data

ISBN 0-8028-0513-2

Design and Typesetting by Vera Brice
Cover design by Leigh Hurlock

Printed by
Nørhaven Book, Denmark

Contents

Preface

In praying and studying within the tradition of Celtic spirituality over the past ten years, I increasingly have been aware of the important place given to matter, whether that be the matter of creation, the matter of our human bodies, the matter of what we handle daily in our kitchens and workplaces, or the matter of the body politic and how we handle the natural and economic resources of our lands. As Lord MacLeod, the founder of the Iona Community in Scotland, used to say, 'Matter matters because at the heart of the physical is the spiritual.' What we do to creation, therefore, what we do to our own and one another's bodies, what we do with the earth's resources is a spiritual issue.

I also have been struck by the similarities between Celtic spirituality and Jewish spirituality, including the beautiful illuminations of Scripture in both traditions. Perhaps I should not have been so surprised to find deep resonances between these two great streams of spiritual inheritance in that Jesus was a Jew, but we have tended to emphasise the differences rather than the common ground. In both traditions there is a radical affirmation of the goodness of creation and of the human body. In Jewish thought the body is the soul in its outward form. In Celtic thought the body is an echo of the soul. It is born and dies, and in that sense is passing like an echo, but it carries within it the sounds of the eternal.

In my publication, *Echo of the Soul: the Sacredness of the Human Body*, I draw on the writings both of Jewish mystics and of great Celtic teachers over the centuries. In both traditions the Genesis 1 description of humanity made in the image and likeness of God is the starting point for spirituality. It is the foundational definition of our souls and bodies, for the spiritual and the material are conjoined. They are inseparably interwoven. In Kabbalistic thought in the Jewish tradition, the human body is like a sacred text in which we may discern the sounds of the soul. Within the body there are shinings of the eternal Self. The crown of the head is associated with the mystery of God's image within us, the centre of the forehead with eternal wisdom, the arms with strength, the heart with beauty, the genitals with creativity, the legs with eternity and the feet with presence. These are like the shinings of the true self to which we are being recalled.

This book is an attempt to utter in prayer what in *Echo of the Soul* I expressed in thought form. The theme of mystery, therefore, is woven into the prayers for the first day, as is the theme of wisdom into the second day, and so on throughout the seven days of the week. In the 'Scripture and Meditation' section for each morning and evening I have included brief phrases from Scripture that can be used as the basis for meditation. In both Jewish and Christian tradition the simple repetition of a biblical phrase, whether spoken or chanted or repeated in the silence of the heart, can lead us to what the Jewish mystics refer to as 'one-pointed concentration', focusing on the presence of God at the heart of each moment.

Sounds of the Eternal: A Celtic Psalter is an expression of the soul. Hopefully it gives voice not just to what is in my soul but to the intuitions and yearnings that are common to the human soul. The depths of who we are as human beings share a birthplace in God. While we may cherish our variously rich religious inheritances, the essence of our being cannot be contained by the boundaries of religion. The soul is neither Jewish nor Christian, neither Muslim nor Hindu. It defies the limitations of any one tradition. As the 14th-century mystic Meister Eckhart says, 'the soul is naked of all things that bear names'. My hope for this book is that it might be used by Jews and Christians, and, indeed, by anyone who is seeking to be renewed in the unity that is deeper than boundaries.

J. PHILIP NEWELL
EDINBURGH

Sunday Morning Prayer

'Happy are those whose hearts do not condemn them,
and who have not given up hope.'

Ecclesiasticus 14:2

Silence

*Be still and aware of God's presence within
and all around*

Opening Prayer

You are above me, O God,
you are within.
You are in all things
yet contained by no thing.
Teach me to seek you in all that has life
that I may see you as the Light of life.
Teach me to search for you in my own depths
that I may find you in every living soul.

Scripture and Meditation

'For you alone, O God, my soul waits in silence,
for my hope is in you.' *Psalm 62:5*

'Those who wait for God shall renew their strength.'

Isaiah 40:31

Prayers of Thanksgiving and Intercession

That you have made me in the image of your own mystery
thanks be to you, O God.
That in the soul of every human being
there are depths beyond naming
and heights greater than knowing
thanks be to you.
Grant me the grace of inner sight this day
that I may see you as the Self within all selves.
Grant me the grace of love this day
that amidst the pain and disfigurement of life
I may find the treasure that is unlocked by love,
that amidst the pain and disfigurement of my own life
I may know the richness that lies buried in the human soul.

Pray for the coming day
and for the life of the world

Closing Prayer

Before me in the planned shape of this day
I look for unexpected surgings of new life.
Around me in the people whom I know and love
I look for unopened gifts of promise.
Within me in the familiar sanctuary of my own soul
I look for shinings of the everlasting light.
Before me, around me, within me
I look for your life-giving mystery, O God,
before me, around me, within me.

Sunday Night Prayer

'In a dream, in a vision of the night,
when deep sleep falls on mortals,
while they slumber on their beds,
then God opens their ears.'

Job 33:15–16

Silence

*Be still and aware of God's presence within
and all around*

Opening Prayer

In the quiet of the night
may I know your presence, O God.
At the ending of the day
may my soul be alive to your nearness.
Amidst the tiredness that overcomes my bod
and the tensions that linger in my mind,
amidst the uncertainties and fears
that haunt me in the darkness of the night,
let me know your presence, O God,
let my soul be alive to your nearness.

Scripture and Meditation

'It was you who took me from the womb
and kept me safe on my mother's breast.'

Psalm 22:9

'You love all things that exist
and hate nothing that you have made.'

Wisdom 11:24

Prayers of Thanksgiving and Intercession

Like light dappling through the leaves of a tree
and wind stirring its branches,
like birdsong sounding from the heights of an orchard
and the scent of blossom after rainfall,
so you dapple and sound in the human soul,
so you stir into motion all that lives.
Let your graces of healing flow this night,
for my soul is wounded
and there is brokenness in my life.
Let your graces of healing flow, dear God,
for those whom I love are in need this night
and there are agonies in the life of the world.
There are agonies in the life of the world, O my soul,
and those whom I love are in pain.

*Recall the events of the day and pray for
the life of the world*

Closing Prayer

Bless my body and soul this night
that I may be renewed in the forgetfulness of sleep.
Visit me in my dreams
that I may remember my birth in you.
Protect me with your angels of brightness, O God,
that I may awake to the freshness of the morning,
that I may awake to You as the new day's freshness.

Monday Morning Prayer

Happy are those who meditate on wisdom
who reflect in their heart on her ways
and ponder her secrets.'

Ecclesiasticus 14:20–21

Silence

*Be still and aware of God's presence within
and all around*

Opening Prayer

In the silence of the morning
I am alive to the new day's light,
alert to the early stirrings of the wind
and the first sounds of the creatures.
In the silence of my heart
I hear the yearnings that are in me and the fears,
the hopes that rise from within
and the doubts that trouble my soul.
In the beginnings of this day, O God,
before the night's stillness is lost to the day's busyness,
open to me the treasure of my inner being
that in the midst of this day's busyness I may draw on wisdom
Assure me again of my origins in you,
assure me again that my true depths are of you.

Scripture and Meditation

'Let me hear what you will speak
when I turn to you in my heart.'

Psalm 85:8

'The desire for wisdom leads to a kingdom.'

Wisdom 6:20

Prayers of Thanksgiving and Intercession

That truth has been inscribed into my heart
and into the heart of every human being,
there to be read and reverenced,
thanks be to you, O God.
That there are ways of seeing
and sensitivities of knowing
hidden deep in the palace of the soul,
waiting to be discovered,
ready to be set free,
thanks be to you.
Open my senses to wisdom's inner promptings
that I may give voice to what I hear in my soul
and be changed for the healing of the world,
that I may listen for truth in every living soul
and be changed for the well-being of the world.

Pray for the coming day
and for the life of the world

Closing Prayer

Like an infant's open-eyed wonder
and the insights of a wise grandmother,
like a young man's vision for justice
and the vitality that shines in a girl's face,
like tears that flow in a friend bereaved
and laughter in a lover's eyes,
you have given me ways of seeing, O God,
you have endowed me with sight like your own.
Let these be alive in me this day,
let these be alive in me.

Monday Night Prayer

'I prayed and understanding was given me,
I called on God and the spirit of wisdom came to me.'

Wisdom 7:7

Silence

*Be still and aware of God's presence within
and all around*

Opening Prayer

I seek your presence, O God,
not because I have managed to see clearly
or been true in all things this day,
not because I have succeeded in loving
or in reverencing those around me,
but because I want to see with clarity,
because I long to be true
and desire to love as I have been loved.
Renew my inner sight,
make fresh my longings to be true
and grant me the grace of loving this night
that I may end the day as I had hoped to live it,
that I may end this day restored to my deepest yearnings,
that I may end this day as I intend to live tomorrow,
as I intend to live tomorrow.

Scripture and Meditation

'Show me wisdom in my inner being.'

Psalm 51:6

'I will show you hidden things that you have not known.'

Isaiah 48:6

Prayers of Thanksgiving and Intercession

For the wisdom that fashioned the universe
and can be read in the earth's dark depths
and in heaven's infinity of lights
thanks be to you, O God.
For the wisdom of teachers before me
and their words and imaginative seeing,
for the wisdom of those I have known
and their silence and humility of speech,
and for wisdom's wellspring in my own soul
and in the soul of every human being
from which ancient truths and new realisations spring forth
thanks be to you.
Let wisdom unfold in my own heart and mind
and in the men and women of every nation.
Let us see the foundations for a new harmony
within us and between us,
the foundations for a recovered unity
with the earth and all its creatures,
for the ground of life is in you, O God,
the ground of all life is in you.

*Recall the events of the day and pray for
the life of the world*

Closing Prayer

In the great lights of the night sky
and its unbounded stretches of space
I glimpse the shinings of your presence, O God.
In the universe of my soul
and its boundless depths
I look for emanations of your light.
In the silence of sleep
and the dreams of the night
I watch for jewels of infinity.
In the silence of sleep
and the dreams of the night
I watch for the shinings of your presence.

Tuesday Morning Prayer

'You lift up the soul, O God, and make the eyes sparkle.
You give health and life and blessing.'

Ecclesiasticus 34:20

Silence

*Be still and aware of God's presence within
and all around*

Opening Prayer

As the day's light breaks the darkness of the night,
as the first movements of the morning pierce the night's stillness,
so a new waking to life dawns within me,
so a fresh beginning opens.
In the early light of this day,
in the first actions of the morning,
let me be awake to life.
In my soul and in my seeing
let me be alive to the gift of this new day,
let me be fully alive.

Scripture and Meditation

'Awake, awake, put on your strength.'

Isaiah 52:1

'Maintain the right of the lowly,
rescue the weak and the needy.'

Psalm 82:3–4

Prayers of Thanksgiving and Intercession

Thanks be to you, O God,
for the stirrings of new life in me this day,
for rising from the dreams of the night
to a fresh flowing of energy,
for the vitality that awakened my body
and the desires that stir my soul.
Let me know the power for life that is in me,
the life-force that is in my senses
and the might that is in my heart.
Let me know you as the source of such force
and be wise to its true streams and false currents.
Let me serve love with my strength this day,
let me serve love with my strength.
In heart and mind and body this day
let me serve love.

Pray for the coming day
and for the life of the world

Closing Prayer

The strength of the rising sun,
the strength of the swelling sea,
the strength of the high mountains,
the strength of the fertile plains,
the strength of the everlasting river
flowing in me and through me this day,
the strength of the river of God
flowing in me and through me this day.

Tuesday Night Prayer

'Heed the counsel of your own heart,
and above all pray to the Most High
that you may be guided in the way of truth.'

Ecclesiasticus 37:13,15

Silence
*Be still and aware of God's presence within
and all around*

Opening Prayer

At the ending of the day,
in the darkness of the night
I seek an inner assurance of your presence.
My body is still
and my soul is silent
as I listen for the renewing springs of your Spirit
deep in the ground of my being
and in earth's quietness all around me.
Guide me to the wellsprings of health
in the landscape of my soul
and to the hidden reservoirs of strength
in the people and places of my life
that I may be made well this night,
that I may be made well.

Scripture and Meditation

'You are the stronghold of my life;
of whom shall I be afraid?'

Psalm 27:1

'You endowed me with strength like your own.'

Ecclesiasticus 17:3

Prayers of Thanksgiving and Intercession

Thanks be to you, O God,
for the strong arm
of those who have given me shelter in my life,
who loved me from the womb
and carried me as a child,
who guarded me like watchful angels
and wept when I was in pain.
Thanks be to you for the men and women
whose passion for the poor is undying,
whose prayer for the oppressed is tender,
whose defence of the wronged is fierce.
Grant me the strength to cry for justice,
to be patient for peace,
to be angry for love.
Grant me the grace of a strong soul, O God,
grant me the grace to be strong.

*Recall the events of the day and pray for
the life of the world*

Closing Prayer

It is in sleeping that my body is refreshed.
It is in letting go that my soul is revived.
It is in dying that I am born anew.
Bless to me my sleeping, O God,
bless to me my letting go,
bless to me my dying,
that tonight I may enter your stillness,
that tomorrow I may awake renewed,
that in the end I may be fully alive to you.
Tonight, tomorrow and always, O God,
may I be truly alive to you.

Wednesday Morning Prayer

'Those who rise early to seek God will find blessing.'

Ecclesiasticus 32:14

Silence

*Be still and aware of God's presence within
and all around*

Opening Prayer

In the silence before time began,
in the quiet of the womb,
in the stillness of early morning
is your beauty.
At the heart of all creation,
at the birth of every creature,
at the centre of each moment
is your splendour.
Rekindle in me the sparks of your beauty
that I may be part of the splendour of this moment.
Rekindle in me the sparks of your beauty
that I may be part of the blazing splendour
that burns from the heart of this moment.

Scripture and Meditation

'Strength and beauty are in your sanctuary.'

Psalm 96:6

'You are the author of beauty.'

Wisdom 13:3

Prayers of Thanksgiving and Intercession

Glory be to you, O God,
for the rising of the sun,
for colour filling the skies
and for the whiteness of daylight.
Glory be to you
for creatures stirring forth from the night,
for plant forms stretching and unfolding,
for the stable earth and its solid rocks.
Glory be to you
for the beauty of your image
waking in opening eyes,
lighting the human countenance.
Glory be to you. Glory be to you.
But where the glistening is lost sight of,
where life's colours are dulled
and the human soul grows hard,
I pray for grace this day,
I pray for your softening graces.

Pray for the coming day
and for the life of the world

Closing Prayer

That in the elements of earth, sea and sky
I may see your beauty,
that in wild winds, birdsong and silence
I may hear your beauty,
that in the body of another and the interminglings
  of relationship
I may touch your beauty,
that in the moisture of the earth and its flowering
  and fruiting
I may smell your beauty,
that in the flowing waters of springs and streams
I may taste your beauty,
these things I look for this day, O God,
these things I look for.

WEDNESDAY MORNING PRAYER

Wednesday Night Prayer

'My soul is satisfied as with a rich feast
when I meditate on you in the watches of the night.'

Psalm 63:5-6

Silence

*Be still and aware of God's presence within
and all around*

Opening Prayer

My genesis is in you, O God,
my beginnings are in Eden,
my origins are those of every man and woman.
Forgive me the falseness of what I have become,
the ugliness and divisions of which I am a part.
Restore me to the truthfulness of my birth in you,
the heritage of all that has being.
Renew me this night in the genesis of my soul,
the beauty of Eden deep in each created thing.

Scripture and Meditation

'Create in me a clean heart, O God.'

Psalm 51:10

'I will make your wilderness like Eden,
your desert like the garden of delight.'

Isaiah 51:3

Prayers of Thanksgiving and Intercession

I have seen beauty of spirit
in a child disfigured by disease.
I have seen gentleness of soul
in a dying woman's calloused face.
I have seen a willingness to be merciful
in the life of a people who have been wronged.
Let these be remembered in my heart this night
as I seek a renewing of life.
Let these be remembered in my heart this night
as I seek a rebirthing in my depths,
as I seek new birthings in the world, O God,
new birthings of your Spirit in the world.

*Recall the events of the day and pray for
the life of the world*

Closing Prayer

In sleep may my body be rested.
In sleep may my soul be renewed.
In sleep may my dreams be carriers of truth
borne by the night's visiting angels.
In sleep may I know you in love, O God,
in sleep may I be known by you,
the Lover of every living soul this night,
the Lover of my ever living soul.

Thursday Morning Prayer

'From the rising of the sun to its setting
the Mighty One speaks and summons the earth.'

Psalm 50:1

Silence

*Be still and aware of God's presence within
and all around*

Opening Prayer

With you is the source of life, O God.
You are the beginning of all that is.
From your life the fire of the rising sun streams forth.
You are the life-flow of creation's rivers,
the sap of blood in our veins,
earth's fecundity,
the fruiting of trees,
creatures' birthing,
the conception of new thought,
desire's origin.
All these are of you, O God,
and I am of you.
You are the morning's freshness.

Scripture and Meditation

'My soul thirsts for you, O God.'

Psalm 63:1

'You shall be like a watered garden,
like a deep spring whose waters never fail.'

Isaiah 58:11

Prayers of Thanksgiving and Intercession

That from my depths new life emerges
thanks be to you, O God.
That through my body
and the bodies of men and women everywhere
heaven's creativity is born on earth,
children of eternity are conceived in time
and everlasting bonds of tenderness
are forged amidst the hardness of life's struggles,
thanks be to you.
That in my soul
and the soul of every human being
sacred hopes are hidden,
longings for what has never been are heard
and visions for earth's peace and prosperity are glimpsed,
thanks be to you.
For those near to me who are in turmoil this day
and for every family in its brokenness,
for the woundedness of my own life
and for every creature that is suffering,
O God of all life, I pray.

Pray for the coming day
and for the life of the world

Closing Prayer

In the gift of this new day,
in the gift of the present moment,
in the gift of time and eternity intertwined, *when...*
let me be thankful
let me be attentive
let me be open to what has never happened before,
in the gift of this new day,
in the gift of the present moment,
in the gift of time and eternity intertwined.

Thursday Night Prayer

'To those who repent God grants a return.'

Ecclesiasticus 17:24

Silence

*Be still and aware of God's presence within
and all around*

Opening Prayer

At the setting of the sun,
in the enveloping darkness of night,
at the interplay of hours
with sunlight giving way to moonlight,
I step from the day into the night
with a desire to be still,
and in being still
to turn to you, O God,
and in turning to you
to return to the creative depths of my soul.
At the setting of the sun,
in the darkness of the night
I turn to you.

Scripture and
Meditation

'With you is the fountain of life.'

Psalm 36:9

'You have power over life and over death;
you set free the imprisoned soul.'

Wisdom 16:13–14

Prayers of Thanksgiving and Intercession

I have witnessed inspiration of spirit
in the voice of a woman,
in the colours of an artist,
in the prophetic vision of a leader,
in the most simple acts of daily kindness and neighbourliness.
I have experienced creativity in my own soul,
in seeing things anew,
in unplanned utterances of wonder and passion,
in the most ordinary actions of tending and caring.
In the life of the world this night,
in every nation and among every people,
let there be fresh stirrings of your Spirit.
In my own soul and in the world tonight
let there be fresh stirrings of your mighty creating Spirit.

*Recall the events of the day and pray for
the life of the world*

Closing Prayer

As earth requires rest
and the seas need time to be replenished,
so in resting may I be made more alive,
so in stillness may my creativity be born anew.
Bless me in the night, O God,
that I may wake refreshed.
With your ministering messengers of sleep
bless me in the night.

Friday
Morning
Prayer

'You make the gateways of the morning and the evening
shout for joy.'

Psalm 65:8

Silence
*Be still and aware of God's presence within
and all around*

Opening Prayer

In the light of the high heavens
and the infinity of dawnings in space,
in the darkness of ocean depths
and the sea's ceaseless waves,
in the glistening of a creature's eyes
and the dark life-blood that ever flows,
in every emanation of creation's life
and the warmth that moves my body,
in the inner universe of the soul
and its everlasting foundations
your glory glows, O God.
In every shining of the world's inwardness
and the warmth that moves my everliving soul
your glory glows.

Scripture and Meditation

'I love the place where your glory abides.'

Psalm 26:8

'Your immortal spirit is in all things.'

Wisdom 12:1

Prayers of Thanksgiving and Intercession

For the life that was in the beginning
and is now
thanks be to you, O God.
For the life that is now
and will always be
thanks be to you.
For those who have gone before me
and the men and women of every nation,
for the vitality of children
and earth's life-forms still to be born
thanks be to you.
In this great river of life
that flows behind me and before me
let me know that I am carried by you.
In this great river of life
that flows around me and through me
let me know that I carry you
and can reverence you in all that has life.

Pray for the coming day
and for the life of the world

Closing Prayer

That your glory rises in the morning sun
and sparkles off flowing waters,
that the glory of the everlasting world
shines in this world
growing from the ground
and issuing forth in every creature,
that glory can be handled, seen and known
in the matter of earth and human relationships
and the most ordinary matters of daily life,
assure me again this day, O God,
assure me again this day.

Friday
Night
Prayer

'The voice of God is over the waters,
the God of glory thunders.
The voice of God flashes forth flames of fire.
The voice of God shakes the wilderness,
and strips the forest bare;
and in the temple all say, "Glory!"'

Psalm 29:3,7–9

Silence

*Be still and aware of God's presence within
and all around*

Opening Prayer

In the temple of my inner being,
in the temple of my body,
in the temple of earth, sea and sky,
in the great temple of the universe
I look for the light that was in the beginning,
the mighty fire that blazes still from the heart of life,
glowing in the whiteness of the moon,
glistening in night stars,
hidden in the black earth,
concealed in unknown depths of my soul.
In the darkness of the night,
in the shadows of my being, O God,
let me glimpse the eternal.
In both the light and the shadows of my being
let me glimpse the glow of the eternal.

Scripture and Meditation

'The whole earth is full of your glory.'

Isaiah 6:3

'You made me in the image of your own eternity.'

Wisdom 2:23

Prayers of Thanksgiving and Intercession

At the heart of life
and in its heights
glory shines.
Within creation
and beyond
glory has its source.
Guide me to the heart of life
that I may know its heights.
Lead me further within, O God,
that I may know you as beyond.
In the sufferings of my heart
and the brokenness of creation
open to me further
the doors of the eternal
that through the pain that is within me
and the struggles that are around me
I may be guided to you as the heart of life,
that through the pain that is within me
and the struggles that are around me
I may be guided to you as in and beyond all that has life.

*Recall the events of the day and pray for
the life of the world*

Closing Prayer

Bless me this night, O God,
and those whom I know and love.
Bless me this night, O God,
and those with whom I am not at peace.
Bless me this night, O God,
and every human family.
Bless us with deep sleep.
Bless us with dreams that will heal our souls.
Bless us with the night's silent messages of eternity
that we may be set free by love.
Bless us in the night, O God,
that we may be set free to love.

Saturday
Morning
Prayer

'Wait for God,
be strong and let your heart take courage,
wait for God.'
Psalm 27:14

Silence

*Be still and aware of God's presence within
and all around*

Opening Prayer

Early in the morning I seek your presence, O God,
not because you are ever absent from me
but because often I am absent from you
at the heart of each moment
where you forever dwell.
In the rising of the sun,
in the unfolding colour and shape of the morning
open my eyes to the mystery of this moment
that in every moment of the day
I may know your life-giving presence.
Open my eyes to this moment
that in every moment
I may know you as the One who is always now.

Scripture and Meditation

'Seek God's presence continually.'

Psalm 105:4

'I am the first and I am the last.
Do not fear for I am with you.'

Isaiah 44:6,8

Prayers of Thanksgiving and Intercession

At the beginning of time and at the end
you are God and I bless you.
At my birth and in my dying,
in the opening of the day and at its close,
in my waking and my sleeping
you are God and I bless you.
You are the first and the last,
the giver of every gift,
the presence without whom there would be no present,
the life without whom there is no life.
Lead me to the heart of life's treasure
that I may be a bearer of the gift.
Lead me to the heart of the present
that I may be a sharer of your eternal presence.

*Pray for the coming day
and for the life of the world*

Closing Prayer

In the many details of this day
let me be fully alive.
In the handling of food
and the sharing of drink,
in the preparing of work
and the uttering of words,
in the meeting of friends
and the interminglings of relationship
let me be alive to each instant, O God,
let me be fully alive.

Saturday Night Prayer

'The crash of your thunder was in the whirlwind,
your lightnings lit up the world.
Your path was through the mighty waters,
yet your footprints were unseen.'

Psalm 77:18–19

Silence

*Be still and aware of God's presence within
and all around*

Opening Prayer

Unseeable
I have seen you this day
in the lights of the skies,
in the green of the earth,
in flowing waters.
Untouchable
I have felt you this day
in the warmth of the sun,
in the wildness of wind,
in the touch of another.
In and beyond my senses,
in taste and touch and sound
your mystery has been made known.
At the ending of the day,
in the darkness of the night,
in and beyond my senses
let me know your presence, O God,
let me know your everlasting presence.

Scripture and Meditation

'As a deer longs for flowing streams,
so my soul longs for you, O God.'

Psalm 42:1

'The mountains may depart and the hills be removed,
but my steadfast love shall not depart from you.'

Isaiah 54:10

Prayers of Thanksgiving and Intercession

In my mother's womb
you knew me, O God.
In my father's birth
and in the birth of his father
were my beginnings.
At the inception of time
and even before time began
your love conceived of my being.
As you have known me
so may I come to know you.
As you prepared my birth
so may I make way for fresh birthings of your Spirit.
As you sowed all things in love
so may your love for all things be born in me,
so may your love be born again in me.

*Recall the events of the day and pray for
the life of the world*

Closing Prayer

The rhythm of life is yours, O God,
the changing of the seasons,
the busyness of the day and the night's stillness,
youth's energy and age's measured pace.
For daylight followed by hours of darkness,
for the time of letting go
and of taking off the clothes of the day,
for the time of lying down
and being covered by the night's intimacy,
for the overlapping of the seen and the unseen,
heaven and earth,
flesh and angels,
body and spirit,
rest and dying and new life
all part of your rhythm, O God,
thanks be to you.

Hebrew Illuminated Manuscripts

The artwork used throughout this book is from illuminated
Hebrew manuscripts now housed in the British Museum Library
in London. The decorative painting and beautiful calligraphy of
Jewish texts, including Scripture and prayer books and marriage
contracts, for example, reached a peak of expression in Europe
between the 13th and 15th centuries among the Sephardic (Span-
ish and Portuguese) and Ashkenazic (Central and Northern
European) Jewish communities. Even as early as the 9th century,
however, in Palestine and Egypt there are examples of decorative
carpet pages at the beginning and end of Hebrew books, consist-
ing of intricate geometric patterns and abstract designs that are
curiously modern in feeling. The striking similarities between the
artwork of medieval Hebrew manuscripts and the considerably
earlier illumination of gospel texts in the Celtic Christian tradition are likely not coincidental. Both of these traditions evidence a
type of family likeness also to Arabic art forms and the illumination of the Koran in Syria and Persia. Clearly there was cross-fer-
tilisation between cultures and religious communities.

The focus in all of these schools of art is the written word. The
art is there to serve the sacred text, to accentuate the mystery and
the power that the word carries. Certainly in the tradition of
Hebrew illuminated manuscripts the scribe was the master of the
artistic process. Usually Jewish, although sometimes a Christian
artist employed by a Jewish patron, the scribe would plan the
layout of a page, sometimes doing the basic decorations himself,
and then oversee the work of illuminators, copyists and appren-
tices. He would decide which words were to be highlighted in gold
and which colours were to be used throughout the text, although
to a certain extent he was limited by the materials available in his
region. The ink was usually prepared from a simple combination

of charcoal and water, and most of the paints were extracted from natural compounds, the more durable ones being a mixture of well-pounded minerals or coloured stones bound together by egg-white and water solutions. The parchment was usually sheepskin, although goatskin, cowhide and calfskin vellum were also used. The result was the beautifully illuminated collections of Jewish sacred texts that have endured the centuries.

With the sacred text being the focus of this art form, often it is initial words from books of scripture or even entire verses that are decorated. This has a way of drawing the inner attention of the reader to particular words, such as 'Give thanks to the Eternal' or 'The soul of every living being'. One of the phrases regularly highlighted in illuminated manuscripts of the Haggadah, the ritual recited in the Jewish home on Passover eve as part of the seder meal, is 'Next year in Jerusalem', referring to the hope for peace in Jerusalem and all that that represents for humanity, both physically and spiritually. Also included frequently are artistic depictions of matzah (the rounded unleavened bread eaten at the Passover meal), suggestive of the Eastern mandala, the sacred circle of the eternal used for meditative purposes. As well as Passover illustrations there is much Temple-related imagery employed in illuminated manuscripts, the menorah, for instance, the seven-branched oil lamp representing the fullness of God's presence of light. After the destruction of the Jerusalem Temple in 70CE, the Bible in fact is sometimes referred to in Jewish tradition as 'God's Temple', the place of epiphany.

One of the most distinctive features of Jewish illumination is the use of minute script, referred to technically as micrography. This consists of words of biblical commentary, fashioned into geometrical and floral designs, that are so minute as to be almost indecipherable. Even the creatures of earth, sea and sky that appear in border illustrations and carpet pages of the manuscripts sometimes bear within themselves portions of minute script etched into their very bodies. This points, of course, to the mystical sense of the 'word' or 'understanding' of God as something that can be discerned in all things, including the creaturely. Like St John in the

Christian tradition it points to 'the Word made flesh', the Word that is heard not by turning away from life but by listening deep within all that has life, by being attentive to the spirit that is inseparably woven into the physicalness of the universe and of every created body. The art form is there to serve the written word but not in a way that takes our eyes away from creation and the human mystery. Rather it draws our attention further and further into the matter of life and of human relationship, recalling us to the Life within all life or to what the Jewish mystics call 'the great shining of the world's inwardness'.

Illuminations used at the beginning of each day

SUNDAY	First word of 'In distress I called upon the Eternal' (Ps 118:5).
MONDAY	Micrography carpet page (The Lisbon Bible).
TUESDAY	Seven-branched menorah (The Farhi Bible).
WEDNESDAY	Matzah and the harmony of the universe (Barcelona Haggadah).
THURSDAY	Six-pointed star (The Golden Haggadah).
FRIDAY	'Hallelujah' from Psalm 117:2 (The Golden Haggadah).
SATURDAY	Prayer words 'Next year in Jerusalem' (Barcelona Haggadah).